HELLO NOBODY

STANDING AT THE DOOR ALONE

What To Do When Everything Changes

Chris, Tell Your Story,

Janet

JANET HANEY

DEDICATION

I dedicate this book to Sarah, my daughter and my friend.

You are the light of my life and have given me the courage to start my new journey.

Table of Contents

"Your heartache is someone else's hope. If you make it through, someone else will make it through, tell your story."

— **Kimberly McManus**

PART 1

INTRODUCTION

Have you found yourself in a place of life transition? These changes can leave you wanting to call out, "hello, Nobody!" to an empty house. That's what happened to me. I found myself suddenly facing life alone, and in circumstances not of my choosing.

The trials of unplanned transition are steep and full of pits and valleys. When faced with heartbreak and loss, no matter the cause, there is a choice to be made. We can keep looking backwards holding onto life as it was, or look up and ahead to discover new possibilities and ultimately a new you.

I have discovered a key to maneuver through these difficult places. I'm not at the finish, but will share the path I took. The harder the trial, the more our faith can be sharpened into a rod of strength, and that makes all the difference.

Any change brings a new beginning. A new start can happen anywhere along the way. It takes being brave enough to realize you're not standing at the door alone.

Here is my story.

CHANGE HAPPENS

"Some stories don't have a clear beginning, middle and end. Life is about not knowing, having to change, taking the moment and making the best of it, without knowing what is going to happen next."

— Gilda Radner

I did not come into this world alone; I was given a womb-mate, as my twin brother likes to say it. He arrived in this world first; ten minutes later I came along. As the family story goes, the delivery doctor proclaimed, "Wait, there is another one!" And I was that "one". My mother was unaware that she was carrying twins. There was not ultra-sound technology back then and being a bit pre-mature, I can see where a mom might not know she was carrying a "pair." I do think my mom might have suspected at some point there were two of us nestled inside her, but it was a surprise all the same.

My brother and I are as different as night and day. He's the dark haired and introspective one; I'm the blond and people-pleasing one. They say twins possess a certain connection that those of single birth don't share. Some even develop a unique "language" that passes between them. We had a special understanding, a bond that went deeper than just brother and sister. We had an unspoken link that I especially felt.

At age seven I was excited to be going to sleep-away camp with my brother. Then, I was horrified to realize the boy's camp was across the lake. It never occurred to me that we would be separated. I struggled and cried the full week, missing my "mate." The cabin counselor, who probably thought I was crying for my parents, was thrilled to help me pack when the week was over and time for me to go home. I was not able to process my feelings at the time; I just knew I was in an unfamiliar place and, despite the camp fun all around me, instinctively there was a piece of me missing.

On the other side of the camp, however, my brother was having a wonderful time, and did not mind that his side of the lake was free from girls. I remember standing on the bank, gazing across the waters, knowing he was over there. It was the first time we were separated for any length of time. He fared well; me, not so much.

Our next parting came at school. Up until that time, we were in the same classroom with our desks side-by-side. We shared a lunch box with images of famous cowboys of the 1950's- Roy Rogers on one side for him, the counterpart cowgirl Dale Evans on the other side for me. I never thought it strange to share a lunch.

I'll never forget the day I was told that the other first grade class needed another girl and I was selected to join them. The teacher used the, wouldn't-that-be-nice approach, and the next thing I knew, my desk was packed up. I was moved across the hall to face a new room, new teacher, and new classmates. Alone. No brother. This yank out of the familiar and comfortable was significant for me. I was "on my own" again.

My brother seemed to prosper as a solo. I, on the other hand, felt the sting of separation. I relied on him for more than just a lunch mate. I never learned how to spell our last name, which seemed a bother. I had always copied from my brother's paper. I no longer had that luxury in my new classroom. Standing in line at the teacher's desk, behind a row of wiggly classmates, waiting to have our spelling words graded, I remember the panic of how I would explain that only my first name was written across the top of my page. I had to think quickly as the line moved and my turn approached. To my relief, a "brilliant" excuse popped into my head. I relaxed, knowing I had my bases covered. Surely the teacher would buy it!

Unfortunately, she didn't.

When it was my turn to stand at her side, the anticipated question came quickly. She asked about my missing last name and my clever answer was at the ready. With newly found self-confidence I replied, "Oh, I don't have one." Astonished by her reaction, I found myself banned from recess to write rows and rows of my last name on the chalkboard. Fifty times, I printed that name.

It worked. Alone in the classroom, I finally learned how to spell my family name, Wilhelmi.

As the years passed, two more sisters came along and when I was thirteen another brother. We were a family of seven, living in a three-bedroom duplex with one bathroom. Living arrangements were tight and small, but we didn't think anything of it.

Before we knew it, my twin and I found our parallel paths diverge into separate places. We parted for College. He the more academic one, had a thirst for learning, especially reading. An English major was a perfect fit. I, on the other hand, struggled more in school. Things didn't come as easily or quickly to me. I tried my hand at several majors, even attending a few different Universities, before settling into a particular field of study. We kept an eye on each other, but life has a way of sending travelers across different bridges to places far apart. My twin and I were not to live close-by each other again. His life took him to other states where roots grew and he raised a family. I know I will always be his twin, even though he's still taller and older by ten minutes.

My path eventually took me to the place where I would meet the man that would take my life on a journey I could never have imagined.

I was the one that answered the phone when this handsome intern—my husband-to-be—called to ask my roommate out for a first date. My roommate and I both worked at the hospital where he was a first year medical intern. I was working as a medical technician, and my roommate was a R.N. We shared a small duplex parked on the edge of the hospital parking lot.

When he asked if she was home, my answer was not what I expected to come out of my mouth. "She's not home, but I'm not doing anything," I responded. I surprised myself with my answer because I was not "that" kind of girl.

The next thing I knew, he was picking me up for a hospital dance we never attended. Instead, we talked for five hours over dinner. That was the beginning and the end—we married when his medical training was over.

By the time the wedding was decided and planned, I had discovered my academic destiny and was finishing my graduate school program in Gerontology.

These were days filled with study and making wedding plans. My middle sister and I always shared a close relationship. There was no way of knowing it would soon become even closer. She met the handsome brother of my fiancé. They fell quickly in love, and as fate would have it, asked if they could join us at the wedding as a second bridal couple. That seemed a fine solution, a double wedding; sisters marrying brothers. It saved out of town family travel time, expense and seemed the practical thing to do.

I shared a wedding and a new last name with my sister.

I was Bride-A as the oldest and she Bride-B. We met our dad at the front of the church and having two brides, escorted us both to the altar. Our other sister was shared as a special bridesmaid for both of us and was much appreciated.

This wedding was the talk of the town and I suspect we had unknown "guests" appear just to witness a sister-brother double wedding!

After the wedding we parted ways; my sister and her new husband drove across the country for a honeymoon and a new life on the West Coast. My husband and I stayed on the East Coast, moving to his hometown.

That was when everything changed... again.

Married life was all I hoped for, and more. My new husband was my best friend. We had a bright future and a solid relationship to get us there. He loved adventure, the outdoors, discovering new and old things and cleared the way for me to open my eyes and life to places and people I wouldn't have otherwise met. I was joined to someone who had the answers to questions, a love for life, and a deep desire to infect the world with his enthusiasm for living and learning.

I was very happy and didn't think things could be better. I should have guessed my sudden "flu" symptoms in the middle of the non-flu season were something more. And they were. My future looked even brighter because I was expecting my own surprise in the womb.

I insisted that we look for a home of our own: one that would accommodate our soon to be growing family. Our rented home was fine at first, but the "mother bird" was coming out and I had a desire to fluff and settle down. My husband reluctantly joined the real-estate agent and me for a Saturday morning "quick look" at one house. The agent had other plans, and the day stretched into an event that included lunch and most of the afternoon. (We actually set off a burglar alarm at one of the showings.) I didn't think things could get worse until getting back into the car for what would be our last house-look for a long time, I realized something was terribly wrong. I was bleeding.

Leaning over, I whispered in my husbands' ear the question no man would know the answer to: "What does it feel like when your water breaks?" In a flash, our real-estate agent drove us madly to the nearest hospital. (I'm sorry to say we didn't buy a house from her.)

That night, our little one was born ten weeks premature and weighing a mere two pounds, fourteen ounces. Truly little, she had to "grow" in the hospital for what would be more than fifty days. She came home on Mother's Day, weighing just over four pounds! Our treasure fit inside a baseball hat and wore the smallest preemie clothes.

Our days were filled with laughing, baby crying, nursing, and precious little sleep. But such is the way with infants no matter their size. She grew and prospered and became the sunshine in our life. I still see my husband holding her as a tiny infant dancing her around the room to the Motown tune of *My Girl* by The Temptations. She was his world, and he was her champion. He found pure joy in our little girl. When she was old enough to take dance lessons, he was the most enthusiastic "dance-dad" as we like to call him. He so enjoyed her recitals and dance competitions, when she was a bit older, he talked of wanting to own a dance competition company. He never missed an opportunity to watch and cheer for his favorite and only daughter.

Two years later another bout of morning sickness gave way to our second child, this time a son. Having never carried a baby to full term before, I felt extremely large and uncomfortable carrying him, and so happy when finally, he arrived! We thought he was a giant at his birth weight of seven pounds, compared to his older sister who weighed just ten pounds when she celebrated her first birthday.

When he was born all things were going along smoothly until I tried to nurse him for the first time in the hospital. I phoned my husband, who was at his office, to chat. As I talked, I looked down to see the baby had stopped breathing. He turned blue right before my eyes! Before I knew it, the transport team from the local Children's Hospital packed my new son into a tube-like isolate and whisked him out of the room and into an ambulance. I would not see him again until I was released from the hospital three days later.

We had no way of knowing we were embarking on a journey lasting nine years.

Our baby's development seemed slow. We had clues early on that he was developing at a different rate than other infants. We only had our preemie to compare him to developmentally. She was mixed-up on her growth milestones, but we still noticed his delay. We tried not to be concerned. However, when he still couldn't hold up his head at six months, we realized he was more behind than we could ignore. We suspected something was not right.

It wasn't.

The doctor reported his development at only six weeks, not six months. We were warned that he might have a seizure problem and to keep an eye on him. What exactly would that mean? What would our lives look like? We had no idea. Soon after, our world consisted of physical therapy, seizure medication, and the immense fear that our baby might stop breathing again. But he grew strong and was a delight. The smallest thing brought such joy to him. He loved insects, especially ants and bees. He prayed at night for them. He loved eating casseroles, and looking at the pictures of food in cookbooks.

By the time he was ready for elementary school, our world expanded to include special school tutors, therapeutic swimming, occupational therapy, and speech therapy. Despite my busyness and intense schedule, I was happy. Being a mom was a perfect fit for me, I felt cut from this cloth. To me, life was as it should be, despite our unique challenges. I felt fulfilled and hopeful for the future of our little family.

Our little son was a joy and we celebrated every milestone of his development, no matter how far behind his age group he remained. Crawling, walking, feeding and talking were all mastered on a timeline known only to him. Our "special" boy brought a dimension to our family that's only fully understood by those who have a "special" member of their own. He marked us, and we became better people because of him. He taught us patience, acceptance, and joy. But mostly he taught us about love and loving unconditionally. His sister adored him and he returned that adoration.

He lived a full life on his terms. He had a sweet spirit

and I'm sure the angels that came into his room when he was nine years old knew those things about him. However, I may have gotten ahead of myself, so allow me to back up a little.

It was a Monday morning I will never forget. Like lots of children, our son didn't know that weekends were for sleeping in. I appreciated his early waking on school or therapy days, but like most parents, I longed to sleep a little longer on weekend mornings. That Monday morning, we slept until 8:00 am—having no little feet stomping into our room at the crack of dawn. I woke thinking, "Wouldn't you know it, a school day and everyone is sleeping in!"

My husband found him in bed. The covers exactly as we left them the night before-just the way he liked them. He was still as glass...and he was gone. That moment, our lives changed forever.

To this day, I wonder why I didn't hear or suspect anything the night he died. Most mothers attest to having a special "ear" that detects stirrings from their children; stirrings that are unheard by others. But I hadn't noticed a thing. They say the loss of a child is the hardest to bear. I agree. It's a crushing hurt that takes all breath away and gives pain that takes up residence deep inside you. As the years pass, fewer and fewer people see the scar that is left behind, inside me, but it is always there. My little boy's life was short but not small. In nine years, he touched many people and accomplished all he was destined to do. In many ways it's not the length of our lives, but the depth, that matters. He had a way of deeply touching hearts and teaching about the real meaning of love. That's a big purpose in life, especially for one so young. His legacy lives on in our hearts.

I believe that God can redeem anything. He can take the sorrow life brings and heal us to be stronger, if we allow it. Deep wounds are not forgotten, and God can bring comfort and peace to raw places, just be patient.

The months that followed our son's death were filled with trying to accept a nightmare. We were all thrown into stunned shock that made the world around us seem dull and foggy. We felt lifeless and hollow. Our family needed to figure out how to recalibrate into a family of three members now. We felt like a table that was missing a leg. We were wobbly and unsteady, no matter how much we tried to prop-up our family. Our missing boy was missing. I don't know how long it took for me to not grab four placemats when setting the table, or to have a strike of pain to look over at the spot that was his place at the kitchen table. These hard days are true in any loss. The holes left by the missing piece is as real as the pain it brings when walking around it.

My husband's heart was so heavy with the sadness of our loss that he finally saw a medical doctor for a checkup. More grief was hiding in the corner. What the doctor discovered was another surprise and a shock. He diagnosed my husband with inoperable Stage Four prostate cancer. He was too young, and the reality of it was too big. Again, devastation hit our family. Where do you pull courage when it seems your tank has not refilled from the last time it was needed just so you could survive. We didn't know how to process this news as the next few months were filled with trying to figure out a medical game plan. We knew we had a long, arduous journey ahead of us.

This journey lasted nearly ten years. Treatment, transfusions, and slow decline finally took its toll and the cancer could not be beat.

There was never anyone who wanted to live life more than my husband. He didn't want to leave us despite the fact he had a peace inside about his next destination. I think God fills us with a longing to stay with loved ones here, but gives the grace to let go when the time is right. My dear husband slipped peacefully into that heavenly place and I am confident he opened his eyes to see our little boy. That is a blessing I hold dear.

Losing a husband brought bigger change than I could imagine. We stood together as a family for so many years only to watch his life decline before our very eyes. When the battle was finally over, my daughter and I were weary and worn thin from the wounds of the fight. And many scars remained.

Still, our struggle was just beginning. You have to fight

to keep going when the world you know is suddenly gone. Losing a brother and a father for my daughter, and a son and husband for me, felt unbearable. We each coped in our own way. Things in my life settled into a quiet roar. The yarn shop I owned kept me busy and gave me a place to belong. The customers and staff filled my life with friendship and purpose.

Then I got the phone call.

The Breast Center asked me to return the next day for a diagnostic mammogram. Don't worry they assured, these things are usually nothing 80% of the time. I knew it must be something to be concerned about, because I am never the 80%. They informed me that I had early stage breast cancer.

Here was another surprise that came out of nowhere, and yet another devastating change. I was not alone; I faced this circumstance with dear friends and my daughter that planted themselves around me. My fight was not as grueling as that of my husband's. I opted for a mastectomy and reconstruction, and am glad to have the ordeal behind me. Losing my husband and son put me in a tender place for God to fill me with strength and peace that I couldn't provide for myself. Only an empty vessel can be filled with new wine. It has taken me a long time and a lot of heartache to know this.

My daughter and I were blessed to have each other close by, as she finished her graduate studies, including a doctorate degree. Hard work has a way of giving direction when life seems to go off kilter. I know there is a very proud dad who smiles at her accomplishment. In due time, she left the area to discover her own destiny and new life. I found myself alone for the first time in my life. I felt as though I was standing in the middle of a crowded room, watching everyone else live full lives of family and purpose, while my life was nothing but an empty shell. Although I looked the same on the outside, on the inside I was still torn and scared.

I needed to find my new place and purpose. So much had been ripped from the soil of my life, I couldn't see how anything new could grow or bloom. Through the garden of close friends, I've come to realize that family comes in all forms. We just need to reach out and pick them.

With their help, I began to pick up the heavy pieces of my life. Still, there are many rocks and boulders left in my way. I suspect the holes left by the ones I love so dearly and miss so terribly will always be present. I know I need to move on and learn how to live around the vacant spaces. That's the challenge for anyone who has had to cope with unwanted transition. It's a battle we didn't choose, and didn't want, and it's easy to give up. I say don't. Keep going. There really is a light through this tunnel of pain and confusion; that's why they call it a tunnel. There's another side.

"Hello Nobody" are words that echo in my ear whenever I walk into places that were once full of life. My job now is to see where my new path takes me. Each step can lead to a new beginning. I'm choosing to focus on that now (as is my daughter), which now leads to the next chapter in my story.

REFLECTIONS

1. What is the Story you need to tell? There is someone that needs to hear it.

PART 2

Change Brings
The Unfamiliar

*"Never be afraid to trust an
unknown future to a known God."*

— Corrie ten Boom

I protect myself with a large comfort zone. I wear mine like a rubber tube around my waist. I manage very well, encased safely in the middle of what I know and understand. When I'm pushed to the outer rings of this safety zone, I feel unsettled and anxious. The familiar makes me feel safe and secure. I'm the kind of person that knows one way to drive to a particular place, and always take the same route. There may be other ways, perhaps faster and more direct, but I go the way I know. That's part of my comfort zone, feeling confident in what I know to be true. Adjusting to change is a hard thing for me, especially devastating change. That kind, hurts and forces us to accept things in our life we don't want; like being alone.

When faced with trying something new, my first reaction is to decline. Perhaps I'm afraid of failure, of getting lost, or of not being able to follow through. That's why it's been so hard for me to start over. I want my old, familiar life. I was good at being a mom and loved being a wife. In my mind that is who I am. But that's not how it is anymore. It doesn't matter what puts a person in an unfamiliar place- moving on to a new city, a divorce, changing a job, adjusting to an empty nest- the heavy heart that is the same. We sit next to each other on the same bench of pain. It feels rough and hard and we don't like it very much.

THE UNFAMILIAR

Loss and change occupy two sides of the same coin. Whenever something is lost, a new thing is sure to follow. It's a relationship that I have a hard time accepting. Yet, if I don't accept this coin, I'll be stuck with my feet in the mud of yesterday.

God Can Make All Things New. Ask him.
He takes the unseen and makes a way.

There are many synonyms for the word *change*: alter, modify, transform, adjust and amend, to name a few. Taken separately, these words are full of promise and power. As a collection, they are transforming. On the other hand, they can seem terrifying. When life throws a curve ball right in the middle of a lovely inning, it can knock you down, hard. Hit with change, no matter what the form, often we're not ready, we're caught with our gloves down and we get hit in the face.

I want these terms of change to become hopeful possibilities for me. I want to see how they fit into my inside spaces. I'm getting ready to plant these words and see how they grow for me. I'm ready to be transformed but I need to visualize a new me.

When I let go and open up, I can discover the new things God has in store for me. I have confidence He knows the places I see in myself. He whispers for me to hear. I want to recognize His voice; I want to accept His plan for the way things are unfolding. I trust that God can make all things new—even the old things, even hard things.

New destinations require that we take action. We have to figure out how to become comfortable with the "new." While the "old" is familiar and comfortable, it takes courage to embrace anything "new."

The unsettling feeling of upheaval or loss of identification is scary. The important thing to know is that it's okay. We don't have to take the journey alone. God, our Father, loves us and will gently lead us to the new place. Forever a gentleman, He will hold every door for us.

I have moved farther and deeper into the unfamiliar places that have opened up in my life and at first didn't like what I saw. There were days when all I could do was crack the door I needed to walk through and peek in. I didn't have the courage to start a journey that seemed unfamiliar and foreign. I had no person's hand to hold, to walk beside me and share this next place in my life. I was now a widow, had an empty nest, and was living with the uncertainty that cancer pours into your world. There is always the small spoken question; will it return?

I am not very brave. I sat in the hallway of my life for a long time. I couldn't go back to the way things were and I was afraid to move forward. It took some time for me to stand up and take some steps. If you are in this place now, don't worry. You will know when it's time to take your stand and face the way things are now. We can do more than we think with a broken heart. It comes along with us, but we can learn how to bandage it by accepting love and support from those around us. It may not be your husband, your child or a parent anymore; it comes from the sweet fragrance of dear friends and family. God plants these blossoms around us when we need them most. Look for them; they are your familiar in an unfamiliar place.

REFLECTIONS

1. Take a moment to camp around these words of *change*. I encourage you to think about the action you see that is needed to take you from the fear of the **Unfamiliar** to the possibility of a New Thing.

   Alter: Is there something you can move to the side right now?

   Modify: What small piece can you adjust to make the unfamiliar, familiar?

   Vary: Is there a new way to do an old thing that will give the same results?

   Transform: Do you see a new a way of thinking or the change of a habit?

   Revolutionize: This is change in a whole new way. Does that seem possible?

   Adjust: This is the first step to taking hold of change...move your thinking to a new place.

   Amend: Is there any place you need to make corrections or is there anyone you need to forgive?

THE UNKNOWN

"One is never afraid of the unknown.
One is afraid of the known coming to an end."

— **Sira Masetti**

I have a terrible sense of direction. I get lost easily, even with MapQuest leading the way. The small voice hidden inside my phone often announces, "recalculating" or directs me to "make a U-turn." In most cases, I know when I'm lost and I don't appreciate her reminding me. But I am thankful when she is able to get me back on track. I wonder about that voice...

Even armed with directions for the journey, it's easy to take a turn and end up somewhere unfamiliar. It results from our own missteps or from life handing us a map that we don't know how to read.

I know what it feels like to not know where you're heading. Many times the road has changed course and I have been forced onto an exit ramp to the unfamiliar. My first reaction is to panic and fear. Things may look the same, but they may not be in the same order or in the right location. I become confused and need help. This disorientation can be brief, just until firm footing is regained, or it can persist for a time that seems to have no end. For me, it's usually the latter.

Life has thrown me a few sucker-punches that I never saw coming. The blows doubled me over and made it hard to stand up straight. My injuries were internal—my heart was broken, my mind rattled, and my legs paralyzed. I was struck hard, then struck again. And yet again. I longed for a referee to call the fight so I could get up and get away. I was left in a heap, wondering "why?".

I know there's a purpose to everything and that it takes courage to recover from life-altering surprises, especially when there's no earthly explanation. I take comfort in knowing that sometimes the answer is that there is no earthly answer, at least not this side of heaven.

We have to be careful not to allow the Unknown to grow roots, like the sucker shoots on a tomato vine that steals sustenance and growth from the new fruit waiting to develop. Even though God sees the new plan inside and has fresh things for us, our impulse is to hold onto the old and familiar, even when it's gone.

Fear of the Unknown steals our strength, and with it

our joy. It keeps us tied to the past making our feet too heavy to travel very far, and forcing us to get stuck. While I want to know where I am going before I head out, God wants me to trust that He knows the way. He wants me to be brave as I step into what for me is uncharted territory. I have to remember that even if the path looks underdeveloped to my eyes, God sees the whole picture. He knows that a garden path will turn into a trail, which will grow into a country lane, and then a highway. In short, He will not throw us on an interstate until He has equipped us to travel safely.

I don't know how it works, but I trust God as King David did when he said,

"But I trust in you, LORD; I say, you are my God. My times are in your hands..." Psalm 31:14, 15. I want my times to be in His hands as well. It takes faith to come to that conclusion and step out into the stormy waterways that look fierce enough to swamp our boat.

There will be times and seasons when we are asked to move along and the road is covered with rocks and sand and not made visible. Sometimes, there is no path shown at all, and the view ahead looks like a heavy fog that strains our eyes to see what is coming next. We walk in the unknown and feel unprepared.

We must accept that progress can be made in small steps at first. The more fear and unbelief we lay down, the more room there is for trust in God to develop. Then we are able to bend down and pick up our next thing.

If my arms are full of my uncertainties
there is no room for God's better way.

For me, I was unfamiliar with being alone. I always had another person; a twin, and other brother and sisters, a husband, great parents and children to camp around my life. When everything changed, I was forced to travel uncharted territory and I wondered if I had the strength to make it. My destination has changed. My life was no longer as I had expected or envisioned.

I've learned that change brings a choice. It forces us to shift our outlook and figure out how to deal with the unexpected. Have you ever found yourself in an I-never-thought-that-would-happen-to-me situation? The bigger the roadblock, the harder it is to confront the issue. Sometimes we have to take it in small pieces. Small bites of acceptance will eventually swallow the whole. But it takes time.

Life is full of the Unknown. How well we fare depends on how we react to the things we don't understand. Although it's a struggle, I'm learning to not be afraid of what the future may bring. There are still days that I don't want to get out of bed and face my new life. But I do and, looking back, I see that I was given all the provision I needed for that day.

God doesn't forget us.

I have had to do some hard things by myself: sell my husband's office building, dispose of the belongings of a late husband and son, move out of the home I lived in for 26 years, build a new house, and buy a car. To me, these represented mountains I had to scale alone because I no longer had someone to help.

Your hard thing may not be anything like mine. A spouse leaving may have you in poverty with few options; maybe it is a phone call with devastating news about your treatment options; or news your company has eliminated your long held position. No matter the unknown territory staring back at you, it is a surprise to discover the strength and understanding that comes, when you need it, not before.

That is how God works. We are given the shoes to climb whatever mountain stands in our way, but not before we start the trek. Sitting in the driveway, looking into the distance to see the struggle that stands in our way doesn't bring any solution.

God waits until we are ready to take the first step. It may be small at first, but then we realize doors open, paths are made straight and circumstances are settled. It's just as He had planned and just at the perfect moment. If this hasn't happened yet for you, don't lose heart. I know God sees the puzzle of your life and the pieces scattered all across the floor. Each section plays an important part in putting the picture back together. It may not look the same as the one on the outside of the box anymore, but a new image.

That's a loving God. He always makes a way, but we have to confidently join Him in the journey.

REFLECTIONS

1. Are there any fears of the Unknown you currently see in your life?

2. Take a few minutes to think about them. Ask God to prepare you for the journey ahead.

The Unseen

"There are things known, and there are things unknown.
And in between are the doors."

— Jim Morrison

Change also brings the Unseen. By that, I mean we have no way of seeing what the future will bring. There are always turns and forks in the road that conceal what's ahead. These twists may bring us to places of blessing and prosperity or to places of hurt and hardship. If we worry too much about the Unseen, our minds and hearts can be shrouded in dread and fear. Fortunately, many of the Unseen things we worry about never do take place.

As humans, we like to know what's next. I know I do. I've been known to read the last few pages of a book first, just so I'll know how the story ends before it begins. For me, there's comfort in not being surprised. However, it is a spoiler and I don't recommend the practice. It's just an example of how I try to avoid an Unseen situation. When it comes to life, we can't control the unseen. You will never sleep if you try, there is just too much to it. So, I say don't try. The way to avoid the worry of the Unseen cropping up in your life is to trust. However, trusting in you, only brings more stress, because we have no vision of the Unseen.

But, God can see it. It's hard to imagine how that works, but believe me, it does. His voice can be as loud as a trumpet, as small as a whisper, or a subtle nudge in your heart. However He comes to you, **He provides the framework that gives sense to a senseless situation.**

God cares about us. He sees each tear, even collects them in a bottle. He cares enough about tears to save them. "You keep track of all my sorrows. You have collected all my tears in your bottle. You have recorded each one in your book "(Psalm 58:8 NLT).

God knows all about crying. Tears burn from our eyes and heart and let sorrow escape. The pain doesn't go away, but the expression of it or the sadness we feel can run down our cheeks. God knows about tears; they are important enough to be noticed. I love the thought of God watching me so closely, He can see a tear drop from the side of my eye. Mine are mingled with yours and it is a comfort to know something as small as a teardrop is not wasted or forgotten. The shortest verse in Scripture says, "Jesus wept"

(John 11:35 NIV).

God can touch that spot inside you that beats the hidden feelings of uncertainty and fear. "Fear not" is a command given often in Scripture. We need to take that call seriously. Take the apostle Peter, for example. He climbed out of the boat in the middle of the raging storm to obey Jesus's call to him to, "Come!" (Matthew 14:29 NIV). Peter's fear of what lies ahead and the unseen danger of raging winds and crashing waters caused him to look down and miss the miracle of the impossible; walking on the water. I'm sure I've missed some great miracles in my life by taking my eyes off the Unseen God and focusing on the rocky circumstances in front of me.

When our hearts are heavy with sadness, any kind of sadness, it's easy to crawl into a shell of isolation. I have been in that corner. My world as I knew it came crashing down, more than once, when my son died and my husband slipped into heaven. I felt as if time stopped for a while after each loss. The world seemed to carry on as if nothing happened, but to me, everything had happened and I was left spinning.

I will never forget spending an afternoon driving around town looking for a cemetery to bury a nine-year-old. The official showed us plots, pointing out the special features, as if looking for real estate. My heart was crushed. I was broken in half and quietly mad. There seemed no point in a child dying.

During these times I found it natural to focus on the volcano of grief that left its mark in all parts of my life. The thick sticky pain of heartbreak clung to me and seemed to burn right through my flesh. I felt disfigured and ugly. I didn't know if the hurt would ever subside. However, I understood that if I stayed here for too long, it would be hard to climb out. Hurt has a way of dragging us down, to our knees.

It took some time, but I decided to change my focus off the pain, off me and my loss. Then I was able to hear the gentle voice of God assuring me He would use this for His glory. I didn't understand at the time what that could possible mean, but years later I have an idea.

My suffering might open the heart of someone else who is suffering. We can look into each other's eyes and see the hurt, because we know. To find someone who understands the things we can't find words to explain, brings a bit of healing and hope. That is what God wants from us, to share ourselves, and in doing so we share His love.

I experienced the marvel of walking through the fires of hardship and was made stronger for it. The astonishing thing was not the hardship, it was the extraordinary presence of God who made himself real to me in the hardship. There is certain learning that's only broken open from the fires that burn deeply.

The Unseen turns that come when life changes course doesn't have to be for the worse. We often perceive these changes as bad because we don't like to leave the familiar, no matter how scratchy that familiar place may be. There is a process to change, a path to accept the New. No one can predict where or how to walk into this place before it's in front of us. Pieces of the old stick to our hearts, sometimes forever, as fragments we never forget. Yet, we must move on. And we do.

REFLECTIONS

1. Do you feel prepared to face the Unseen things up ahead?

    a. Whatever fears are gripping you, acknowledge them and then denounce them. They will no longer control your future.

    b. Tears play an important part in our human condition. Visualize the bottle God fills with yours.

THE UNWANTED

*"When a train goes through a tunnel and it gets dark,
you don't throw away the ticket and jump off.
You sit still and trust the engineer."*

— Corrie ten Boom

Change is always hard when it is unexpected, unplanned or unwanted. Of course there are some good forms of change to be celebrated such as a new baby, a marriage, or a promotion. The stress associated with these positive changes is outweighed by the joyful event.

However, the type of change I am talking about in this book is the unwanted kind—the life change that takes on a grief all its own and seems impossible to swallow. It's bitter and may be a silent devastation known only to you. No matter what it is, your life has been altered.

Such heartbreaking changes can be paralyzing and confusing. They can knock you off your feet and break your spirit. This kind of change can leave huge chunks of despair that you can't get your heart around, or the smallest of glass shards that cut deep and are impossible to remove. No matter the size, you have to live through it. You can't skirt around it. We have to deal with the unwanted change that stares us down from the middle of our path. Even if we close our eyes and pretend it isn't glaring back at us, we must act and react. We can't hide, and it will not run away. But how do you do that? How do you put one foot in front of the other every day or just to get out of bed? Unwanted changes take a toll on everything; our health, our relationships and our heart.

The first task is to catch our breath. Just breathe! This is no small task—situations that collapse our lungs of acceptance need time to be restored. It hurts just to breathe and it's okay if shallow breaths are all you can take. There are times when we must sit for a while to let the room stop spinning. This is the time to lean on the sturdy ones in your life. God has already placed them beside you. He put them there to be His hands to hold you. Let them.

Accepting the Unwanted things in life take courage and strength. You may not feel very brave or strong, but if you got out of bed today, you've already proven that you are. That simple act takes courage. Life may seem a blur, as if someone spilled water on your homework and all your well-crafted sentences have faded into a wrinkled and blurred mess. Everything is confusing and mixed-up. When it happened to me, I wanted to jump into a hole. Some days it seemed as if I had.

The trouble with unwanted things in life is often we have no choice. Events happen, decisions are made, loved ones leave our lives and we have no ability to stop it. No matter how fierce we look standing on the railroad track of change, with our arms flailing and our voices raw from screaming for someone to pull the brakes, if the locomotive of change is headed your way, it will flatten you. Those were hard days of struggle and deep sadness for me.

I had a friend who saw those places inside me, and she wouldn't let me stay there. Her solution was, "Let's go hit something!" So we took up tennis together. That was a healing thing for me. We joined a tennis league, and I took beginning lessons. I was not very skilled, but that didn't matter. For a few hours I was out of my house, around other women, and could swing a tennis racket with all my might. Hitting the tennis ball gave my silent pain a small portal of escape. This newly found outlet lasted for a few years and was part of my journey to peel myself back into my life.

I also tried my hand at painting. Again, something I had never tried before was offered as a hand up and I took it. For almost two years, a group of friends met in my basement for our painting group. We were mostly all beginners and coaxed the one who had prior painting experience to be our teacher. We settled into a Tuesday routine of standing at our easels, to paint. At first, each one selected the subject of her own choosing. Then we decided it would be fun to all paint the same thing, and that's what we did. We started with the obligatory fruit bowl still life and progressed to copying the painting styles of some of our favorite artists.

We tried our hand at the painting style of Georgia O'Keefe when I realized how healing this weekly group was for me. Georgia O'Keefe has a very distinct painting style and is one of my favorite artists. She is known for large paintings of flowers that extend to all corners of the canvas. Our group set a vase of creamy white lilies on the table and decided to try our hand at painting our own Georgia O'Keefe style.

These were precious times of healing for my dark moments. For the next few weeks, we camped around our own paintings, giving encouragement and enjoying the process of painting our flowers. It was an easy place to paint every week, as our works in progress could be left undisturbed in various states of completion. Since the death of my boy, there was no more playing in the basement. His toys, close by, left as a reminder to me of simple joy, now gone. It was a silent place for our works of art to rest until we returned.

It wasn't until one day when I scurried down the basement stairs to retrieve something I cannot now remember, that I was stopped in my tracks. There, set up in the semicircle around our table of creamy white lilies, was my painting. I had never noticed in all the weeks we spent painting this particular piece how strikingly different was mine, from the rest. The others painted from what they saw. Each painting was a creamy pale copy of the still life we set before us. Mine was not.

My painting of the flowers was bold with orange, red, deep pink, and purple. My style was thick with paint and not delicate at all. I realized, I was looking at the flowers we were painting, but my heart was choosing the palette, not my eyes. I was painting from my place of hurt and sadness. I didn't feel creamy and white inside, instead, I was orange, red, bruised and bleeding! I didn't realize until almost at the finish of my painting, how different my work was from the others. If they noticed, it was never mentioned. Maybe, they didn't know how raw I still felt inside, but my brush found the way to give me a voice.

The painting group has long since disbanded. The years we spent working together will always hold a special place for me. I still have my crazy painting of red, purple and orange lilies as a reminder that our heart knows our pain, no matter how we push it down.

I am here to encourage you. Don't make the mistake of thinking your life is over—it's not. Yes, it will be different from the life you knew, but God will equip you with a prescription to see clearly again. You just have to be willing to be fitted for the new glasses. His eye exam takes time, acceptance, and trust that He sees what we can't. What God does see is a person healed and whole, even before we are. He knows our potential and wants to raise us up from our place of sadness and fill us with His healing love. Ask Him to show you how much he loves you. He will. Then, God will put you next to others who need to know that also.

The losses in my life have made room for new people to sit beside me. Together we find ourselves in a similar place of accepting an unwanted change. It doesn't matter how the life shift appeared; widowhood, divorce or any loss, a space for something new has opened up inside us. We see that place in each other, we have common ground to stand on.

The unwanted life changes we share put us together in a similar boat. We each have a new destination. As we float towards our own recovery, we'll share seats with those who have been assigned to sit next to us. It's possible we wouldn't have ever met if not for the change in our lives that put us beside each other. God plants them to sit beside us because we share similar experiences and understanding. Look for them—they are all around you. They will bless and nourish you.

Welcome these new friends with open arms—they will help form a steadfast framework to calm and support you. They might be old friends. Friends you knew before your devastating change that will invite you to sit beside them in their pew of heartbreak. You might not have realized their pain before, but once you sit side-by-side and join hands in your suffering you realize you are not alone. God works like that. He designs a place for us to land, long before we need it. He orchestrates circumstances so that there are people for us to sit beside who understand our journey.

If we let the One who sees our today and knows our tomorrow lead us, our unwanted days will become more bearable. God wants to lead you to your next place.

Let Him!

REFLECTIONS

1. Are the unwanted changes in your life keeping you from taking hold of what is next?

2. How can you find others who have been destined to come alongside you now?

3. We can't take back the things that have been removed from our life, but we can trust that God will find treasure in the way we move forward and take another with us.

THE UNPREPARED

"When we are no longer able to change a situation,
we are challenged to change ourselves."

— **Viktor Frankl**

After fifty days of visiting my first little one in the hospital, I had only one hour to prepare for her homecoming. I didn't even have diapers! She only weighed a little more than four pounds. I had been told she couldn't leave the hospital until she reached the five-pound mark. Their rational for an early-weight dismissal was, "It's Mother's Day!" And it was. Fifty days of practice, and here I was on my own with a baby that was too small to fit in an infant car seat. I was unprepared.

Some things in life are impossible to prepare for, even when the thing is expected. When these things actually happen, we're taken by surprise and shocked. I felt that way when my husband died. For nearly ten years he suffered with prostate cancer. Although treated with medication and maintenance chemo for years, the cancer refused to surrender. My husband's decline was slow, but sure. Toward the end, his body thin and racked with pain, I remained convinced he would pull out of the downward spiral and be healed. I was sure a miracle would come. The longer it took in showing up and the frailer his body became, the more evidence I saw for a miraculous healing.

He spent two weeks in the hospital. He didn't want to leave us; we didn't want him to go. Although we had years to prepare for this good-bye, we didn't know how to say it. We were still unprepared.

When I look back on my desperate prayers for a miracle, I realize that my daughter and I did get a miracle that day. It just wasn't the one we were looking for.

God gave us the grace to say good-bye to the rock of our family—the one who cherished us like no other. The moment he slipped into heaven, God lifted us into the palm of his hand and held us close. That was when the miracle happened. We survived another devastation and, somehow, were made the stronger for it.

The ability we're given to climb yet another loss came as we made the trek through the circumstance. It was as if God changed our shoe style of faith, the steeper the terrain became. At first, a light-walking sandal of trust was all that we required. We were concerned about the diagnosis of cancer, but felt confident the treatments would eventually restore my husband back to health. These were days of investigating and making decisions.

When the treatments were not progressing as anticipated, the path became littered with unsteady loose gravel of disappointment and our feet began to slip. The climb became steeper. My doubts were turning into fear about an unseen cliff up ahead. We needed sturdier shoes of faith. The trail was getting more difficult.

Looking back, over each twist in the hike of this journey, my daughter and I were provided larger and deeper faith to keep going. When my husbands' battle came to an end, I realized we were wearing the protective climbing boots that gave us the grace to let him go. He had made the climb through all the suffering and pain, we made the climb as well. We had the view from the summit, and now needed to make the harder journey back down, to pick up the pieces of what life would be like without the one we loved dearly.

That's when the miracle we were counting on all along happened. I realized we were the miracle. The circumstance that wanted to bring us to our knees and throw us into a pit of lasting grief and despair enlarged our hearts. That gave us a tender heart to see the suffering of others. We felt the breath of God in our lungs and were able to keep going.

We're given the ability to walk through circumstances even if we're not prepared. Things I never thought I could bear happened. I didn't always deal with them gracefully or efficiently, yet I dealt with them all the same. I learned that there was more depth to me than I had realized. This kind of understanding only comes from doing something you're not ready to do. There are some things that can only be done with God's help. When we have no strength or ability, He steps in.

Being unprepared for change doesn't have to be as devastating as the death of a loved one, or the crushing blow of divorce papers. Whatever the vehicle, it takes its toll as we struggle to reorient ourselves in a place we feel like we no longer belong.

Unprepared-change changes us!

Looking forward, I see some glimpses of new things peeking out from around the corner for me. I don't know if I will take a deeper look to see where these things lead or not. For now, they're unknown possibilities. As it appears closer to me, I'll decide if it is something I want to pursue or not. It is an unknown now, but has the possibility to unfold into a new thing.

I decided I didn't want my days filled with emptiness when I look into my future. I decided I must step onto the train that will take me somewhere new. Once aboard, I'm committed to discovering new destinations and a new me. I must be willing to imagine what the new me will look like.

Right now, she is up ahead, I can see her form, but she is not in clear view yet. I'm working on that. I want to see the new me. I want to visualize what she will be like. However, I realized there were some "good-byes" I needed to say to feel okay moving ahead. I have never ventured to the grave site where my son and husband are buried. I always told myself, I didn't need to go because they are not there. True. But in looking forward to what this new me could possibly look like, I think I do need to make a trip over to the cemetery. I need to sit for a bit, and say the words, "good-bye." I will take them with me to where ever I travel next, but I need to let them go. That's when a new beginning can come.

I want to embrace the changes that present themselves. I may look the same on the outside, but on the inside, I want to clean the dust and debris left from the struggles I've been through. I want to see a new me. I've learned valuable lessons born from the deep places that were hard to walk. I will share these lessons with any traveler who comes along weary from her own battle.

REFLECTIONS

1. Are you facing, or have you ever faced, anything that has you feeling unprepared?

2. What have you learned from facing this unprepared scenario?

3. Do you agree we can be vessels to help those on the same journey who are feeling the same way?

4. Can you imagine what a "new you" would look like?

PART 3

Change Makes
New Challenges

"Don't be afraid of challenges.
Let them take you somewhere new."

— Sira Masetti

I never thought of myself as having a competitive spirit. I tend to think of myself as more of a quitter than a fighter. The adage: "When things get tough, the tough get going" doesn't describe me. When things get tough, I want to walk away. I know this is a broad overstatement that isn't true for all things, but challenges tend to make me uncomfortable and I find myself looking for an escape.

I wish I were more like those who thrive on challenges, pushing up their sleeves, jumping in, and facing any battle, large or small. They get the job done. My competitive spirit only comes out in simple activities such as board games, water drinking competitions, and ping-pong. When it comes to life, I need a long time to process before I'm ready to act. I like to "talk it through" and have others alongside me for encouragement.

I thrive in a group environment. I love thinking up new ideas, plans or parties, hosting dinner parties at the drop of a hat. I am the only person I know that has more than six sets of dishes, stemware for 40 and a drawer full of over 35 placemats. I live alone. I enjoy cooking and creating a comfortable environment for others.

Everything is different for me now. Maybe for you as well. I turn around in my mind and can remember my house full of people and busyness. Our lives intersected in many places and I was the ringleader. I kept track of all the activities and did a pretty good job. I have learned there are times to step into the water and swim through what's thrown down in front of me. However, I look for a raft before I see a shoreline of a solution. I like to float around the situation for a while. I need time to process what is going on, I don't think quickly on my feet.

That's how I'm wired. God puts circuits inside each of us so we are uniquely one of a kind. At times I feel as if some of my wires get crossed...I am still a work in progress.

There are rough edges of fear and doubt that come along with who I am. He sees the potential. There are layers that get polished smooth by the rock tumbler of circumstance, and that draws me closer to God's side.

The dictionary defines the word *challenge* as something that needs a lot of skill, energy, or determination, especially something never done before. I'm facing the challenge of picking up the pieces of my life and setting them in a new order. Although I've already had some years to restructure and recalibrate the way my life is now, I continue to notice the missing pieces. When my son died, as devastating as that was, I was still a mom and a wife. My life changed, but not my roles. Losing a husband, meant accepting change on a whole different level. I lost a big piece of my identity. Married, I walked in step next to his full and productive life. I was part of it. I was his other half, and he was mine. Now that I am solo, I only have my half of the identity. That is my challenge, to fill in the spaces of my life my husband filled with me. It requires me to expand, to make my world as big as it was before, and do it by myself.

The path of change, which brings challenge, is well trodden with travelers who are further along and just up ahead. I see them all around me. They're strong and help make me stronger by encouraging me to keep going. We need each other. We carry a heavy load that comes with change. When I come home to an empty house now, I'm the only one that feels the depth of the quiet that fills each room—it's thick and heavy. I cut it with music, the company of the evening news, or sitting down with my knitting. I'm learning to adapt and to be okay with the way things are.

With time, you'll learn how to reorder the chaos of change or the quiet that's too loud, in your life. At first you may not know where to place your feet. Everything may look rocky and unsure. Keep your faith that things will eventually smooth out. A new routine will grow, no matter how faint the evidence now.

Trust in Him

Keep moving ahead and trust that God sees where you are and understands your journey. I expect there are days when God tires of me continually telling Him about my situation. But in our constant dialogue, I know His ear is turned toward me and He is listening. I know He hears each thought and silent cry for help and understanding. God is my steady companion and always by my side.

A close friendship is what God desires with each of us, one that is personal and dynamic. It is possible and just a prayer away. If you feel far away from God now, He is whispering your name through your pain and hurt. God is the one who fills us with His love and healing. We can draw inner strength from our own well, or His. We are empty; He is not.

There's no better time to call on the God who sees all and knows us by name, than when we're broken or in need. He came to save those who were lost, and does an eternal job of it. "For the Son of Man came to seek and to save those lost" (Luke 19:10).

God finds us where we are and fills in the gaping holes with His healing touch. All we need to do is ask Him to seal His life inside ours and we're made new. That's the challenge really, to believe this God who stands at the ready, or to trust our own way that's filled with ultimate emptiness. His forgiveness is real and His arms ready to tuck us under his wings to lift us up and set our feet on steady ground.

I chose to be filled by Him and that has made all the difference. I can see the new shoots budding in my life. I'm not fully bloomed as my life continues to unfold. I must confront living alone, missing my children, my husband, married life and friends, and find a new way. I have new people in my circle and am blessed by the gift of them. They have come along to help fill in the places left empty.

No matter where you find yourself now we all face the same challenge. The choice boils down to these: stay the same, live looking back, or pick up the future that waits. I've lived in each of those spaces, some for a longer amount of time than others. Each has its' own comforts and soft spots but also dangers and new challenges. Some days I am not quite ready to move out of the past or afraid to enter the present. The future seems a wide jump and I'm afraid to make the leap. So I don't. I'm content to sit down and imagine what is going on across the divide.

I'll never know what possibilities are waiting, until I go to that new place. Although, the dilemma is there are times that I don't want to go.

I have some years under my belt to restructure and re-calibrate the way life is now. I still notice the missing pieces. That's the challenge; I have never done this before.

God is my steady companion and always by my side.

You'll understand how to reorder things in your life that are out of place as time settles in. At first, it's as if we don't know where to go. Everything looks confusing and we feel unsure. Things do come together, and a new routine grows, no matter how small the evidence.

My relationship with God has become a tender thing to me. It started by asking Him to come into my life, and clean out the mess of sin and take up residence. His presence is a reminder that I am not empty. My life is worth the heart-aches I must endure. The place of pain that breaks me in half is just the spot God wants to touch in me. He fills those places with healing and helps me move forward. It is my choice, yours too. I say if you haven't taken this step, it is the only one that works.

It is easy to say, "Embrace this new challenge!" even when it's the last thing we want to do. However, sooner or later we have to act on the challenge to build a new life out of the ashes of the old. The courage to do so comes from inside. Healing shows up in small steps. But, if we attempt one step each day, no matter how tiny or how long it takes, we do move forward.

TIME MARKS US

Time takes on new meaning. Days, months and years pass and mark the walls of our heart. The doorway in my parents' house is full of pencil etchings and dates measuring the yearly growth of my youngest brother. It's remarkable to see the inches he gained in growth each year. That's the way we are too. Little by little we stand a bit taller in our new place of understanding.

It wasn't until three years after my son's death that I could face emptying my little boy's dresser. I resisted giving up his clothing. They stayed folded just as they were, a reminder of who he was. As mom's we know each shirt and sock. We bought them. To pack them up and give them away represented too final a good-bye. Although sad and painful, there came a time when it seemed right for that monumental step. I did it. Again, we're given the courage to do hard things when the time is right, not before. We have our own private timeline.

Life's challenges have a way of maturing us, not in the

old age way, but in wisdom and understanding. We gain insight when our perceptions shift from just knowing the pain of a situation to taking action to dismantle it. These hard things can glare with eyes of taunting waiting for us to take the first bite of acceptance, and that can be a bitter swallow. It's a process and takes time.

God knows how to refine pain into value. He knows how to take layers of heartbreak and disappointment and polish them to reflect His brilliance in our lives.

That's what we become, God's treasure. Don't waste your challenges; give them meaning by realizing they can become stepping-stones to a deeper walk with God. The time is right for that, no matter where you find yourself.

REFLECTIONS

1. What Challenges are staring at you now?

2. Do you have a plan to chip away at one of them?

3. Have you found others that are facing the same struggle that you can stand next to?

4. Is there something you need to do when the time is right?

New Understanding

"To God belongs wisdom and power;
counsel and understanding are his."

— Job 12:13

Understanding changes everything. It doesn't necessarily bring solution or a desired result, but it gives a situation a place to sit in our heart. It helps us get our mind around a circumstance even if we don't agree with the framework it provides. Our understanding may not be complete. Knowledge helps us feel in control, even if we're not. It helps us accept or come to terms with a problem or heartache. However, that doesn't come easily or quickly.

Sometimes, understanding has to grow from a small seed and the clarity it brings can be cloudy. The dim view we have presently is often all we're given until Heaven reveals the puzzle piece. I may be looking for all parts to fit together, but they're not for me to find. The unfinished piece is all I am supposed to see.

God explains that pretty clearly when He says,

"We don't yet see things clearly. We're squinting in a fog, peering through a mist. But it won't be long before the weather clears and the sun shines bright! We'll see it all then. See it as clearly as God sees us, knowing him directly just as he knows us!"

— 1 Corinthians 13:12 MSG

We must learn to accept that there may be a situation that makes no earthly sense and there is no rhyme or reason to it. These are the hard nuts that sit in the soil of our faith. God will sometimes enrich this ground by not allowing understanding to germinate because He has the understanding, and we don't.

There is growth He wants for us in not knowing or understanding all the pieces. It is called **trust**. When we have a situation or circumstance figured out and tucked into the place we think it should be, we don't need God to lean on. We have ourselves, that's not enough. God, who sees the beginning and the end at the same time, has much better understanding from His perspective. We're so limited in our point of view yet, so often think our view is better.

God gives understanding. It may be partial knowledge

now, but it's steady and comes attached with the ability to accept and grow. He never wastes pain or heartache. That's often the thing He uses to call us to His side, where we can know Him better. Our circumstance can be used as a vehicle to come alongside another person who is marked with pain as we are. The suffering that has touched my life gives me a tender eye to see the same soft spots in you.

Understanding is a precious thing. It is a gift that doesn't fix things, but can smooth the way for us to take steps to a new place. That might be to accept the way things are, no matter how long it takes. They say time heals all wounds, but actually time alone doesn't. It may move us farther away from the particular painful circumstance. However, the sore wound remains until God touches it. Healing can occur without our understanding of the "why?" or "how?" that rides alongside and won't let go. God will soften the rough places where the debris of pain remains. He is gentle and always a healer.

Fortunately, our understanding will come. The response might be as simple as, "I don't understand" and that's okay. That kind of acceptance is a powerful determination. The inner peace you're given to accept the answer that doesn't make earthly sense is a beautiful example of faith. That's believing something that you can't see, but you know is true.

That is just what God loves to see. His children taking such big leaps of faith only He can catch them. His arms are open; don't be afraid to be healed by having a lack of under-standing. The purpose is often not ours to see. It might be for another one to notice that you survived such a blow and you're still standing. Albert Schweitzer once said, "Anyone who has had pain is obligated to help someone going through pain."

I need you to come alongside me when I'm walking through a trial. I need you to encourage me and be patient as I learn how to pick up the shattered pieces of my life. I know you understand, because you have survived your own heartache. I can see your faith in your struggle and that strengthens mine. God will lean us up against each other and we're both made stronger. Look for me, I need you.

If you're still in the place of trying to catch your breath, feeling weak and lost, don't lose heart. That's part of the process. Step out and look up, you're not alone.

PICK UP YOUR MAT

I want my life to be as it was before. I want to see my son grow into manhood, and not have his life end so abruptly. I want my husband to be at my side making plans for our future together. I don't want to carry breast cancer over my head and I want my daughter to live next door. Is all that too much to ask? Yes, it is. Those things can never happen and I know it. I have trouble letting go. But the reality is, life has a way of twisting our plans and paving a whole new sidewalk. The only option is to step up and keep walking.

I want to see my new life up ahead, and reluctantly put my toe into those fresh waters. Some days I'm afraid to commit a whole footstep to this unfamiliar place. I don't want to go there alone. I've left behind my well-known life before everything changed. The memories are neatly folded and packed into suitcases in my heart. I'll take them with me, no matter how far I travel up ahead. I might be farther down the road than I give myself credit, but I am still on the journey.

There are choices to be made. We must decide that life as it is now, is as important as the life we have left behind. It may look different and feel scratchy as an old wool sweater, but I know the more we wear it, the more comfortable it will become and the better it will fit.

Time is a precious thing and days pass more quickly now than ever.

As a kid, Sunday afternoon dragged as if to never end. Not so anymore. I'm astonished at the speed at which days pass. It's as if they are hurricane strength and I'm knocked to the floor. We are given only so much time on this earth, and I don't want to waste the years I have left. My dad was of the opinion that at birth our time clocks were wound, each person given his or her unique allotment of time to live. There is no way of knowing in advance the years we have. Some last a long time, some only nine years.

One thing I know is that there is more I am destined to do, and so are you.

God is in the business of hearing our cries.

I want to be brave. That is a hard pill to swallow and I choke on the size of it. I'm not a brave person. But courage fills me when I need to stand up and show it. I know it's not from me, but from God. It is His shadow I stand under which is protection from the blasting sun of disappointment and fear.

Our only chance to find the life we are to have now is to "take up our mat and walk."

We can sit on the sidelines for only so long, then it is time to move, to stand up and put weight on the new legs of our life. Those places will feel weak and shaky at first, but with use, they will become stronger and stronger. Small steps of doing a new thing are as important as the grander ones. I depended on my husband for many pieces of my life to all fit in the right places. He was a firm wall to lean on and he became part of my balance. I stood straighter and taller because I had his strong points all around me. When all that was gone, I was left trying to catch my balance as if standing only on one foot. I had to learn to trust putting weight on both of my feet and taking steps away from the wall that once held me up.

At the start I felt as wobbly as a new colt, taking a first few steps, unsure of the strength of my legs. I didn't know if they would hold the weight of the grief and sorrow in my core. At first, they didn't, and I would fall to the ground in a crumpled pile of tears and frustration. I felt very alone. I know now, how much that was not true. I can look back and see God didn't miss my trail of tears. He took them and mixed them with his love and made a new wall for me to lean on. Only this wall for strength and understanding was God himself.

God was there for me, even when I didn't realize it.

It's easy to feel alone when life changes beyond recognition. I felt the deep impact of my situation the evening I walked into my now empty house after a long day working at my yarn shop. I called out the greeting, "Hello nobody." Knowing there was no longer a family to meet me, this small shout-out gave voice to a deep place inside me. There was no one to respond to my call that I was finally home for the evening. The dark house gave no sign of life until I entered it. I came to realize that my presence was enough. I could walk into a room, a house or my life and turn on the lights to shine for others to see. I was enough, and being alone didn't necessarily make me lonely.

We can be alone physically, yet never be alone on the inside. That's God's design. He wants to be the wall we lean on and rest up against. God will strengthen the weak places inside us that have shattered and come apart.

He gives solid ground for us to walk, even if the road is filled with pot holes and gravel. The way is made just smooth enough for our feet to follow His footprints up ahead. Walk where He has cleared the way.

Ask God for the understanding you need. He will give an answer or give you the peace to not know. The Bible reminds us that, "And the peace of God, which transcends all understanding, will guard your hearts and your mind in Christ Jesus" (Philippians 4:7 NIV).

Inner peace is a better deal than just having understanding. Peace is calm water that can see the shoreline, no matter how far away or how stormy the waters seem.

I choose that.

REFLECTIONS

1. Is there something you are dealing with that lacks understanding now?

2. Do you think you could trade understanding for peace?

3. Peace will set you free to do what you need to do. It might be to forgive, accept or lay something aside. Ask God to show you how it works for you.

New Places

"Faith is to believe what you do not see;
the reward for this faith is to see what you believe."

— Saint Augustine

I have moved from the North to the South to the Midwest. Each region has its own charm and character and I settled well into every place. The moves I made were always with family. As a kid, my dad changed jobs after coaching at the same college for 20 years. Moving from one city to another came in spurts until I married and settled down in my husband's hometown. That was a season of transition into a new life as a wife, daughter/sister-in-law and later a mom.

This new place was not like the others I had lived; I entered the life of a large family as my husband had 10 siblings, most living in close proximity. Those living out of town came back at regular intervals. The new place soon became familiar. I belonged to that family for 26 years. I was afraid the death of my husband would move me aside as not an authentic family member any more, but that didn't happen. Their arms were wide and many, and that has helped keep me when I was floating in times of rough waters.

The new places I find myself in now are not where I live, but are inside me. I have a small river rock sitting on my dresser. Its irregular shape is evidence of the pressure and tumbling through time and glaciers it took to form it. In black permanent marker I have written the words, **weak made strong**, as a reminder and a statement to myself that my weakness can be used as my strength. Our culture sees any kind of weakness as a fault. We honor strength and power. It's confusing to think power can come from weakness.

The Apostle Paul boasts in his weakness when he writes, "For when I am weak, then I am strong" 2 Corinthians 12:10 (NIV). He suffered an unrevealed affliction that plagued him for his life. We are not told the nature of this suffering, only that it gave reason to give glory to God because of it.

I have come to realize the power of God can rest on me in my weakness. He will become my strength and makes me strong. The words I wrote on my river rock can be yours as well. God will refine us through our trials and give new places of strength inside us. In our weakness we can be made strong. My weak places can't be seen from the outside. They show up as frustration and fear. I know I can step on the heads of these destructive feelings if I turn them over to God who shines His strength on them and they lose their power over me. That makes me strong.

I have stepped up and taken hold of chores and tasks that were formally left to my husband. As anyone, suddenly solo knows, the smallest circumstance can crumple us like an empty can. I remember shortly after my husband died, I needed to set the alarm clock to wake at a particularly early hour. For the life of me, I couldn't figure out how to set the alarm. He always took care of that. As silly as it seems now, that frustration sent me to a place of crumpled tears. I threw the thing across the room. I have since conquered the clock, but have encountered hundreds of things now left for me to do.

Change has its shake ups. The older we become, the more changes appear, no matter the place we live. Time has a way of moving things around. Children grow up and walk their own path. Parents age and need more and more help and care. We realize it might be too late to accomplish some of the things we dreamed to do. Time changes things. What once was an opportunity, may no longer be an option. That's when we learn the lesson of transition. We move from one thing, to the next in action or thought. Like it or not, the only option is to accept the change and adapt to the new place life gives us.

We turn a corner and must keep walking even into uncertainty. That makes us brave, ready to endure what is up ahead, no matter what.

I have faced trials I never thought could be endured. I made it through, and you will too. We are designed to withstand weather that heads our way. Just when the squall is too fierce or powerful, our inner strength rises up. We may be beat down for a time, but God's hand reaches very far to help us stand again.

Change knocks us into new places, like a cue ball breaking set and scattering the neatly racked balls across the pool table. Some land softly in corner pockets, some left in disarray and confusion waiting for the next strike. New places bring upheaval, change, and loss, which then causes us to step away from what we know, to something yet to be discovered. I have learned to stand on shaky footing.

When my legs feel as if they will give out, is just when God wants to show up in ways I don't even realize. His voice is soft and arms strong to hold me when I start to slip into places that are dark and downward. That's a dangerous direction to head and the climb out slippery.

Don't let your sorrow get so deep that you see no way of escape. Have faith to know that there is a bigger picture with parts you can't know. Believing that God was in control, is what kept me from that slide. I didn't understand what was going on, but I trusted God's promise.

"Cast all your cares on Him, because he cares for you"

— Peter 5:7

As heartbreaking as it was to lose my boy at age nine, deep down I had the assurance he was in someone else's hands that loved him more than I did. That kind of comfort comes with the acceptance only our Heavenly Father can pour into a broken heart. However, it took time for my head and my heart of faith to come together. I knew my son was in a "better place" but I wanted him back. He was just a little one with his whole life ahead of him. My heart was torn open and raw. The pain and shock pulverized me. But I survived. And you will too, no matter what you are facing.

God sends new breath in different forms to be part of His healing. I found myself accepting invitations to try all kinds of first time endeavors; activities that brought new friends into my life. Some were only for a season, used to bathe me in the warm waters of laughter and encouragement. That let some of the hurt escape, and gave room for healing to start. Little by little, as I opened my grief pocket, God was able to drip more peace and acceptance into my wounded heart. That helped me release thoughts of fear and panic about the future. We have no way of knowing what lies up ahead. All we do know is, "Be glad for all God is planning for you" (Romans 12:12 Living Bible). We can be confident He has a plan, and wants to share it with us. The trials we have endured can be blended into a future and our new thing. God didn't cause our heartaches, but they can be mixed into the sand of our future to help make a strong mortar that binds us to His side.

HOPE IS LIKE A RESERVOIR

The repair God brings to us softens our desperate thinking. His healing gives us eyes to see the pain in another person. We know how devastating a broken heart can be no mater the cause, because we have one too. As we move along the pathway of healing, God gives us His gift of hope, straight from his heart. Hope is a word filled with layers of meaning. I'm not speaking of a hope as a wish or a hope-so feeling. Biblical hope is not an emotion. It's not a well wish for a nice day. The hope associated with faith in God is a strong anchor to His heart.

> *"Now faith is confidence in what we hope*
> *for assurance about what we do not see"*

— Hebrews 1:1, NIV.

The assurance mentioned in the Hebrews scripture above is the key. God gives us unmatched confidence even in the face of uncertainty. Hope, like faith, can't be shaken by a situation we see with our limited sight. An unseen God can be found in the faithfulness He grows inside us because we have been witnesses to His faithfulness. God can fill us with a hope in the future because He sees the future.

This kind of hope becomes our supply, or a source where God's love can pool around our life and give it a purpose we couldn't design on our own. There is an endless supply stored where we cannot see it. It takes trust to believe God has His hand on the wheel; we just need to let Him drive.

God's reservoir is full of hope and healing, tailor-made for you and for me. It's uniquely equipped to fill us with exactly what we need. And it never runs dry.

It's possible to know this unseen God, as a friend and savior. He has been my framework for the years I have known Him in a personal way. That encounter happened for me when I was sixteen. I remember calling out to God and asking Him to show me if he was real or just a name in the Bible. He answered my prayer, gave me proof in my heart, and my life has never been the same since. I see now even back then, God was preparing me for the things up ahead. I believe He knew all about the change and loss I would encounter. He didn't cause my losses, but had arms ready and waiting to catch me when the time came. I can react to things in a way those without faith in God or biblical hope can't understand. My mindset is rooted in God. He is stability for me, the rock I needed when my life hit a landslide. God has a way of making all things new, even broken people.

Believing God has a plan for each of us is the start. We can trust Him, no matter what. That's where New Places really begin, inside us, with God walking next to us. Our sight is limited, but we can have confidence and hope in the One who knows us by name.

"But those who hope in the Lord will renew their strength. They will soar on wings like eagles; they will run and not grow weary, they Will walk and not be faint"

— Isaiah 40:31 NIV

God gives confidence that there is a plan to life and fills us with hope. The purpose we are designed to have in life will include new places we might not want to go. But we venture into those places anyway, and that makes all the difference.

Let's go!

REFLECTIONS

1. What *New Places* do you see inside you?

2. Do you believe God has a plan for your life right now?

3. What is the first step you must take to accept the *New Place* you find yourself in now?

NEW BEGINNINGS

*"The bamboo that bends is stronger
than the oak that resists."*

— Japanese Proverb

Looking out the window at winters bare trees it looks as if all life is gone. It seems all at once, the warmer days and nights of spring unlock the life that has been resting inside. There is a new beginning, as branches and leaves wake up to fresh life and color. Every ending has a new beginning. Our world is programmed that way.

Change happens and there is no way around it. And just as in *New Places*, how we handle a new thing makes all the difference. We can be bitter and resentful, or hurt that circumstances aren't as we wish. Some people have a harder time accepting change than others. Oftentimes, it requires bending and flexibility.

When my daughter was in kindergarten she came home to realize I had rearranged the living room furniture. She was so upset by my efforts she hid under a blanket until I put things back as they were. She doesn't like change.

Some people thrive on change. They find certain satisfaction in picking up and doing something new. We all need a fresh approach to our routine once in a while. A new haircut or set of dishes, for example, can produce happy results. Change can bring something that fits better, is more up to date or a nicer color. There's some change that I appreciate because it makes me feel accomplished and satisfied. When I finished cleaning out my closet, I kept going back to take a look at the well-organized shelves. There was a feeling of new order. It was pleasing to me.

Then there is the change that devastates. I know about that one; maybe you do too. It's a sucker punch in the gut kind of change. Even when you know it's coming it can throw you down and doesn't let you up. Your world comes crashing down in an instant.

I knew my husband was dying for a long time before he finally let go and left us. We didn't speak very often of what we both knew was the inevitable. I don't know why. I would give anything now to know what he was thinking and how it felt to walk the trail towards eternity. It's certain, we all will march through an ending, but I was just not ready to accept his journey there.

I was certain that door would be shut before he got to it, just at the last minute, and the miracle of his healing would be a wonder to all. I held out for that healing, although it didn't happen. He slipped through the door to eternity one February evening quietly, with eyes seeing what we could not until it is our turn.

Death has a way of changing everything for those who remain behind. We must learn how to live around the hole left in our heart and life, and that's a tall order.

But that's what life is all about: taking hold of what is absent and making the best of a new recipe.

That was the start of a new beginning for me. A new start will come to you from your place of difficulty, as well. The seed of it was planted the moment the change happened. As healing takes over and your footing gets steadier, you will notice a little something inside you that was not there before. Maybe it's the courage to venture out, or not cry for an afternoon. Germination of your new self will begin, with a variety of bloom.

I was afraid if I left my old self and life behind it would somehow diminish me. I was not ready to have a new life. I didn't want one, but one was handed me. Accept it or not, it was the way things were to be.

Every ending has a new beginning.

I am a few years down the road in this journey of a new beginning. Where do you find yourself? Maybe you haven't even taken a journey of life altering change yet, but you will someday. Your kids will be grown and turn into their own life, a job may end expectedly or as a surprise, or the person you thought would be there for life exits yours for another. We can't be prepared before these things actually happen. Just know, when your new beginning comes along, you are not alone. The path is well worn with thousands of stories greater than mine, of courage and comfort. Our stories are what mark us as survivors!

I've realized as I'm sharing my story, the strength we gain is in the telling. Our circumstances are as different as we are, yet similar. A story always has a beginning, a middle and ending. We are like that as well. The start is not where we finish.

We may think the road has a certain destination, a place we are designed to go, but along the way, change happens. The walk becomes unclear and hardship makes travel difficult. The only thing to do is just keep walking. Keep taking steps. In hurtful times, in joyful times, keep walking through the change in your life. There is purpose, often unknown to us. We can't see the plan. We underestimate the maturity that comes from a journey marked with suffering or trials. Whether we know it or not, we are each in the process of writing the story of our lives. There will be powerful chapters of courage and strength in the midst of change. In addition, your tale will have a share of drama and heartbreak etched onto pages we wish could be eliminated. But, these are the events that give depth and texture to a life story, and make it one to be remembered.

Our life stories shine as a powerful tool to light the path of those who are following behind us. They see a shadow up ahead, and know they're not alone.

Allow a negative circumstance to be the sunshine that breaks open the spot in you that needs to change. If you're full of bitterness or unforgiveness, roots grow. These branches will choke out a place for healing or any opportunity for a new beginning. God works in the process of time. In this season, don't miss the lesson you're destined to learn, or be trapped by the snare of despair. That becomes such deep swamp water, no refreshment can be given. It's an easy place to drown. A new you is just under the surface, ready when the time is right to take your past, mix it with your present, for a bright future. No circumstance is missed by God, especially painful ones.

Your story, no matter where it starts, can be the spark of encouragement for someone else. Tell your story. Tell it to yourself, then share it, so we can be part of your new beginning.

Reflections

1. New beginnings happen all the time; it's the life altering changes that take our breath away. How have you taken hold of the situation that changed your life?

2. Do you see yourself as the "Bamboo that bends" or the "oak that resists"?

3. Do you see any roots of bitterness or unforgiveness starting to grow in you? What can you do about it?

4. Have you started to tell your story? How?

A NEW ME

*"How else but through a broken heart
may Lord Christ enter us?"*

— Oscar Wilde

Life has defining moments. These are situations that touch us in some significant way and propel our lives in a new direction.

A defining moment may turn your life in a direction not realized until looking back. It is only then you see the impact a certain thing had in influencing a present or a future. I took an elective class in college, thinking it sounded interesting, but had no particular curiosity in the subject. That single class opened up a new passion I didn't realize was inside me. I ended up earning a Master's Degree in the very subject matter of that class. I didn't know at the time I stepped into a defining moment that turned a corner in my life.

Motherhood is a defining moment. All at once, a new role and new purpose are attached to your side that never leaves. And you are given a new definition. We all have had hundreds of these encounters both small and large, that form the destiny of our lives. They take us to people and places we have no way of realizing at the time, will have a hand in shaping us. Defining moments can have a negative effect if the decisions or people attached to it aren't good for us. I'm sure every addict never intended for their life to be driven by the mad craving that sears through their brain. Now they are defined by it.

Consequently, I feel defined by the circumstances in my life, especially now. There are two ways to look at things: define myself by what I am not or by what I am. I own a yarn shop. I realize now, it was part of the provision made for me years before my husband died. The shop was well established, had moved to its current location, inside a little house. It was a soft place for me to land when the earth shook me off my foundation after he died. Knitters are a unique lot. We have a sixth sense for all things fiber. We will drive many miles in any direction to find a new yarn shop with the excuse of, "its' just up the road." Any fiber-husband has heard these words. There are many quotes about buying yarn, or stash, as we like to call it. One of my favorites is, from *The Yarn Harlot*, Stephanie Pearl-Mcphee, who writes, "**SABLE-** A common knitting acronym that stands for, Stash Acquisition Beyond Life Expectancy." That seems to say it all, and any serious knitter feels the same way.

We understand we can never own too much yarn, and it can be stashed in all corners of the house. There is an instant bond between those that share this passion. No matter where you find yourself, if you are knitting and another of the same persuasion appears, there is instant rapport. We love yarn, we are interested in new patterns and we care about each other. We are a community.

My shop community surrounded me when my husband died and I was grateful. It gave me a place to return and belong when I felt ripped from my life.

So, for now, being a shop owner is big enough. There might be other things I explore or venture into, but that's change I only see in the unseen future.

My grown daughter has become my cherished friend and we stand together even though her life has taken her far away from home. I once defined myself by the roles I played and that suited me. My identity was as wife and mother. You may have roles in your life that shape how you see yourself. We play many parts, and they change as circumstances flow in and out of our lives.

I've had a hard time letting go of this identity. Even as a widow, I wore my wedding band because I was not ready to remove the symbol that proclaimed I belonged to another.

For years I portrayed something that was no longer true. I finally removed it, now all that remains is a permanent indentation on my left ring finger of the promise I once made.

I want my life to be full of people and activity and places as it was before. If you are sitting next to me on this bench, the question I would ask you is: **What should we do about it? How can you have a full life?** The solution is a journey I am still walking. I am heading down a path and making some progress.

The answer is simple and very difficult to achieve all at the same time.

The solution is to take my eyes off me. I realized when my gaze is constantly inward seeing only my pain, my loss, my change, and my grief, I keep walking in circles, gazing downward. For years I have been chasing my tail of sadness. This has gotten me nowhere. For a long time, I defined myself by the pain I have suffered. Everything was colored by loss and grief. I looked fine and adjusted on the outside, no one could see the pain that I took everywhere. I actually got pretty good at hiding it or pretending it was not camped down inside me, refusing to let go. But I knew it was there, and some of it still is.

I realized the only way to get myself back on track was to turn my gaze upwards to see God and ask Him to help me change my focus. I did that. It happened with a prayer of brokenness; broken dreams, broken life and broken heart. I wanted to take off the garment of grief I had been wearing for so many years as it was getting heavy.

God is showing me how to replace my grief with acceptance and peace. It happens, slowly for me because I was comfortable with the fit of sorrow. I knew it was time to change coats when I heard a customer refer to me as, "the sad lady." Wearing the wrong clothing in the wrong season stands out. I made the choice to try on something new and ask God to show me how to take off my sadness and put on some joy.

Everyone told me time heals all wounds. I don't think that is necessarily true, because the pain inflicted by some injuries can't be ignored. Physical or emotional hurt must be dealt with. The truth is, loss, disappointment, rejection, disapproval or any other pain hiding inside you takes a toll and we suffer wounds often unseen by others.

There are fiery arrows full of regret, grief, or despair that take aim and make a direct hit, piercing our heart and mind. If these arrows are not removed properly and the wounds not tended to carefully, an infection of bitterness and anger will set in and damage our spirit.

No one can see our inner pain, but it wounds deeply the tissue of our life. It speaks loudly and brings confusion, giving a place for sadness to grow roots. It hurts.

I am speaking as someone who has encountered these

arrows. They hit me hard and not just once. Each time I was struck with a new swipe of grief, the weapon went deeper into my heart making for a bloody mess.

I decided I didn't want to be raw and bleeding on the inside. I wanted to heal, but how? Time was marching away from the events that caused me pain and it wasn't leaving. I came to the conclusion I must be doing something wrong. I went to counseling. That gave me a chance to talk about the turmoil going on inside, and gave some understanding, and that was a good thing. But the pain didn't leave. I knew I was dealing with something bigger than I could handle. There's a saying that God doesn't give us more than we can handle, not true. My accumulated hurts were too big to handle, alone. Then I realized that's where I was making my mistake.

I couldn't heal myself.

I realized the usual methods of healing pain were not working for me. Counseling, waiting for time to pass, or ignoring the pain in my heart couldn't give me what I needed. I required healing from the inside out. And God was the only one that could mend me.

I was trying to heal myself; my eyes were focused so intently on each slice of my pain I was missing the bigger promise. "The Lord is close to the brokenhearted and saves those who are crushed in spirit" (Psalm 34:18).

God's guarantee is to carry us through no matter the

weight of the pain. Sometimes it is just too much or too heavy for us. It crushes us into scattered pieces that seem to never go back together. I realized I couldn't be pieced together as before. The only way to heal was to let my shattered places be reshaped and fit back inside me in a new way. God has the tools to make the fine chisels and cuts that insure each new piece is reformatted to fit just as it should. He makes me new from the pieces of my old shattered self. That's how we are healed.

We are made new. It's a process and it takes time. However, it's not the time that heals us, it's the procedure of letting go and being willing to take a chance that there is a new way to see life and yourself. There are many lies floating around out there and inside our heads that haunt us with the untruth that we can't change.

It is easy to blame ourselves for circumstances we had no way of controlling. We can constantly compare our life to those around us, and believe the lie that because of what has happened to us, we are somehow not equal to them any longer. We can easily isolate ourselves thinking we don't belong anywhere. The lies go on and on. They can easily take hold and become the new way we frame our lives. Believing a lie, doesn't make it true. These falsehoods can be carried inside us, settling in and live for a long time.

We believe the situation that causes so much pain is my "lot" or my "fault" and that is not the truth. In this brokenhearted place, it's easy to feel as if no one else can understand or relate to your inner pain. These false "reasons" are whispered to you, as truth. It sounds very convincing when feeling so broken and disjointed. The trouble is, if we believe it, the weight of those lies attaches to us and becomes so heavy we lose hope that things will or can get better.

But life can get better. I am on that path. Our ability to change thinking, actions or attitudes doesn't happen overnight. The path starts out very narrow and feels like a tunnel so tight a footstep hardly fits in. I felt squeezed when I started my journey towards healing. There were many things I didn't want to let go from my grip of the past. I didn't know what was up ahead. I was afraid. The past is really all we know to be true. But, as I opened up my fingers one at a time, my load lightened. God is in the business of truth. The things I needed to drop were holding me back from seeing I had a future, let alone a new bright future, just ahead.

God spoke quietly and in circumstances that helped move me along. I am still in motion, still heading to where I need to be. I am not at the finish yet, but I can encourage you to keep going too. God has new things for us just as important as the things we have lost or don't need any more.

My days are still up and down. One day I do a good job of embracing my life, the next, I find myself turning around trying to run back to find what is no longer there. That's when I must sit on the curb of my memories; cry for a bit, then pick myself up and head back to where my life is now. Each time the walk back gets a little shorter, evidence of the progress I've made.

We are the weak made strong, but not by ourselves. We can't talk or think our way into this inner strength. The only way to have real change is to let God move into the place inside you that is hurt. He touches it, heals it and makes it new. Then He moves to the next hurt spot and the process continues.

"So do not fear, for I am with you;
do not be dismayed, for I am your God.
I will strengthen you and help you;
I will up hold you with my righteous right hand."

— Isaiah 41:10 NIV

I can be strong when I am armed with a friendship with God and His hand is on my life. You can have that too. Just ask Him for it.

God has a heart for broken people. He can show us our desperate need for Him through the cracks in our life. Then He can seal us with His love. He fixes shattered people and is good at it. We have no concept of the many things He wants to show us, teach us and give us. It's unlimited, because He is unlimited in love, blessings and gifts. When our dreams are taken away or never seem to work out, God is still there to pick us up and smooth out the wrinkles that deep disappointments bring.

I see how God can use tragedy as a powerful tool to give other people hope that they can make it through the pain of any circumstance, because I did. I am still doing it. The authority we possess because we have made it thus far is a remarkable thing. It gives us credibility and influence. I've had said to me, "Losing a child is the hardest thing to bear, and I could never do it."

If she needs to, she can do it. I know because I have done it. It's a nightmare and one I hope no reader has to ever experience. But if you have, you know what I mean when I say, "We play the hand of cards in life we are dealt." We can't know the hand that will be given to us in advance. There is no way of preparing for the worst, if you can't imagine the worst. The only things to do is have your faith at the ready to stand next to God who sees it all, and believe He will carry you through...no matter what. He did it for me.

Isaiah, a prophet in the Old Testament tells us,

*"The Lord has anointed me...to comfort all
who mourn, and provide for those who grieve
in Zion-to bestow on them a crown of beauty
instead of ashes, the oil of joy instead of mourning,
and a garment of praise instead of a spirit of despair"*

— Isaiah 61:1-3

What God is teaching us here is that He will use the pain we have in life and turn it into a treasure. Wounds and scars are seen as so valuable and so worthy that God treasures them. They can be powerful tools to help others who are as wounded as we are. Pain is never wasted. God will use it to draw us closer to him and teach us lessons that can never be understood outside the crucible of suffering. He has a tender eye to see our bruised spots and heal them. Then we develop a tender eye to see other peoples' hurt places. That's how He uses our scars and wounds: to help us become His hands and feet to serve fellow broken reeds.

> *"A bruised reed He will not break, and a smoldering wick He will not snuff out"*
>
> **— Matthew 12:20**

In my brokenness I have realized a friendship with God that's deeper than it could be if my road wasn't littered with grief and heartbreak. I had a choice. I could let the lies of Satan and arrows of despair take up refuge in my heart and turn me away from God and his healing love. The other option was to run to His side and lean on Him as if nothing else mattered.

That is what I did. I ran to Him. He has become my provision for all that has been taken away in my life. "For I know that through your prayers and God's provision of the

Spirit of Jesus Christ what has happened to me will turn out for my deliverance" (Philippians 1:19).

The Apostle Paul is writing these words from prison chained to a soldier. No matter his circumstance, he prayed for other people continually and needed the prayers of his friends. He encouraged others even when he found himself in horrible conditions. He was looking at the bigger picture, not just at himself.

There is a new beginning waiting for all of us. No matter the suffering you have experienced in your life, God has a plan to use it for His glory. He will strengthen you and and give you wings to soar to know Him in a more profound way.

This kind of new beginning has great value attached to it.

The hotter the flame of life you walk through, the more precious the metal that's developed. Gold, for example, comes from a place buried deep in the earth called, load deposits. The greater our pain, the greater the load deposit we carry. The mined oar passes through a machine called a crusher that pulverizes the rock to release the gold particles. I have felt crushed by the weight of my losses and never thought anything precious could come of it. It takes a hot fire to melt away the impurities that attach to the gold, over one thousand degrees Fahrenheit. God loves us enough to refine us into a thing of greatest value.

*"Behold, I have refined you, but not as silver;
I have tested you in the furnace of affliction"*

— Isaiah 40:10

*"But he knows the way that I take; when
He has tried me, I shall come out as gold"*

— Job 23:10 ESV

We have become gold in God's eyes. We are precious and His treasure.

My Hello Nobody has turned into Hello Somebody...I am becoming somebody new, and in God's eyes it is gold.

It can happen to you.

My new story is just beginning. I don't know where the path of my life will lead, I only know I'm ready to take steps and venture out of the safe place I've kept harbor for the past few years. I will try new things, travel to new places and be brave enough to trust that my life still has a purpose and a plan. A new thing doesn't diminish the life I leave behind. It will always be with me and has molded me into the person I am today.

You will know when the time is right for you to open the door that stands in front of you. For some, a new beginning is a quick and smooth transition. Others must ready themselves over time and accept change step by small step.

Either way, we are God's treasure for withstanding the trials and tribulations life has thrown into our path.

My prayer for you is that your, *Hello Nobody,* season will give you a time to reflect and know that God is in the business of healing broken hearts and He puts us back together in order to make us new. We don't need to Stand at the Door Alone.

ABOUT THE AUTHOR

J anet owns a yarn shop in Kentucky called, Knitwits Contemporary Yarn Shop. It was a soft place to land when life gave her unwanted changes.

Janet discovered life may never be as it was before, but found strength and deeper faith from the trials and heartbreak she has walked through. She has a grown daughter who lives in Colorado Springs.

She writes a weekly blog post in the Knitwits Yarn Shop newsletter that reaches over 1,700 people.

Contact Janet Haney at: HelloNobodybook@gmail.com

35101091R00067

Made in the USA
Middletown, DE
19 September 2016